A Passion For Pilates

Nishant Baxi

pencil

ISBN 978-93-5883-072-9
© Nishant Baxi 2023

Published in India 2023 by Pencil

A brand of
One Point Six Technologies Pvt. Ltd.
Unit no. 26, Ground Floor, Building A1,
Wadala Truck Terminal Road,
Near Post Office, Antop Hill, Mumbai - 400037
E connect@thepencilapp.com
W www.thepencilapp.com

DISCLAIMER: *The opinions expressed in this book are those of the authors and do not purport to reflect the views of the Publisher.*

Author biography

I am an experienced content creator and digital/social media marketing professional with a demonstrated history of working in the publishing industry. Skilled in E-Learning, Market Research, Online Advertising, Management, and Business Development, Content Development.

CONTENTS

What Is Pilates.. 5

Beginning Pilates 9

Beginning Mat Pilates.. 12

Props and Equipment for Pilates 15

What is Contrology... 19

Pilates for Rebuilding Strength and Flexibility.................... 23

Pilates - Exercises and Benefits Part One........................... 27

Pilates - Exercises and Benefits Part Two........................... 31

Pilates - Exercises, and Benefits Part Three 34

Pilates - Exercises, and Benefits Part Four 37

Pilates - Exercises and Benefits Part Five 40

Pilates - Exercises and Benefits Part Six 43

Who Should Not Do Pilates 47

Pilates for Pregnant Women 51

Pilates Resources 55

Appendix 58

What Is Pilates

The Pilates Method, more commonly known as Pilates, is a popular kind of physical activity and exercise that aims to improve the body's strength and flexibility.

Pilates began early in the 20th century. Joseph Pilates, a German boxer and circus performer who, during World War I, was forced into an internment camp, developed it. While in that camp he developed floor exercises to help keep himself healthy and rehabilitate his fellow detainees.

After the war, Joseph Pilates came back to Germany and trained the Hamburg Military Police for a short period. He eventually moved to the United States, where he met his wife. The two of them worked together to improve the Pilates method and invent special equipment.

He trained students in a studio in New York, who eventually became teachers of the Pilates method. Some teachers chose to teach Pilates in its original form, while some teachers opted to include their styles, creating a contemporary style of Pilates.

Joseph Pilates wrote two books on Pilates. The books are entitled "Your Health: A Corrective System of Exercising That Revolutionizes the Entire Field of Physical Education" and "Return to Life through Contrology."

Joseph Pilates initially called this exercise Contrology. According to him, Contrology is the principle of controlling the muscles of the body with one's mind. This is the main element of Pilates and is necessary to be able to create a fusion of mind and body.

Joseph Pilates developed 6 Pilates principles, namely centering, control, concentration, precision, breathing, and flow. To gain the maximum benefits from Pilates, a practitioner should practice all these principles.

Centering

Centering refers to the process of directing all your energy to the center of the body. This center, which includes the abdomen, hips, and lower back, is known as the powerhouse area. Pilates believes that a strong center is crucial. From this center, all other movements flow outward.

Control

Control refers to the process of keeping all the movements thorough. Complete control must be exerted on all muscles of the body. This ensures that the body is in the proper position, preventing injury and leading to effective results.

Concentration

Concentration refers to the process of focusing your mind on every movement. Full attention is given to even the slightest motion of the body.

Precision

Precision refers to the process of ensuring that the body is in the proper form. Every muscle should be where it should be because every movement is accomplished for a certain purpose. Pilates focuses on the quality instead of the number of movements; thus, fewer but more accurate movements are employed.

Breathing

Breathing refers to the process of inhaling and exhaling fully while doing the exercises. This is accomplished so that the body's circulation is improved and that the waste products are removed completely from the body. All the movements in Pilates are coordinated with breathing.

Flow

Flow refers to the process of doing the Pilates exercises fluidly. Every movement is connected to the next, and no movement is static, isolated, or jerky. In Pilates, grace is more important than speed.

Benefits

Pilates has been known to lead to various health benefits. Pilates increases flexibility and balance of the body. It also promotes an increase in height by properly aligning the spine, resulting in better posture. Lung capacity is increased and body circulation is also improved. The body also becomes stronger, specifically the powerhouse region. Aside from a form of exercise, Pilates is also being used in rehabilitation.

Disadvantages

Pilates also has its disadvantages. Pilates classes are usually expensive, as the cost of a class includes payment for the studio, specific equipment, and the instructor.

Also, there has been an issue regarding the certification of Pilates instructors. Shortened training programs at much cheaper costs have resulted in poorly trained instructors. To respond to this need, an organization called the Pilates Method Alliance was formed in 2000. This international organization maintains the appropriate standard for Pilates training and ensures that trainers are qualified. The organization also developed the National Certification

Exam for Pilates.

If done correctly, Pilates yields a lot of benefits. It is thus important to choose the right trainer to guide you. Pilates makes you more aware of your body, allowing you to gain better control of it in your daily activities.

Beginning Pilates

When starting with Pilates, the first thing you have to do is find out where you can practice. Different places are offering Pilates classes and training sessions. These include fitness clubs, health clubs, recreation facilities, wellness centers, gyms, dance studios, rehabilitation facilities, and even specific Pilates studios.

Group vs. Individual Pilates

Next, determine whether you want to practice group or individual Pilates. If you don't have the time to fit a Pilates class into your schedule or if you just want to practice on your own in the comfort of your home, then it may be better for you to practice individual Pilates. However, it is still recommended that you take a few Pilates classes before practicing on your own at home so that you can be sure that your body is in the proper form and that you are properly doing the exercises.

If, however, you find that you want to engage yourself in a group activity, then group Pilates classes may be ideal for you. Some centers offer a free introductory mat Pilates class to give you an idea of how Pilates works. If you want to undergo intensive training customized to fit your goals, one-on-one Pilates with a certified Pilates instructor may be suitable for you.

Pilates for Rehabilitation

At present, Pilates is being utilized in physical therapy at different rehabilitation and sports medicine clinics. Recent research has shown that Pilates is effective in rehabilitating injured patients, allowing them to return to their normal functioning faster. Pilates is also being utilized in the management of chronic pain brought about by various medical conditions, such as multiple sclerosis and scoliosis, among others.

Preparing for Your Pilates Class

Once you've signed up for your Pilates class, you now have to prepare for your class. The best workout to start in Pilates is a simple mat workout. Mat exercises are generally done on the floor with no or very little equipment. Mat exercises are useful in teaching you the basics of Pilates, and can be used by any person of any fitness level.

Things to Bring

You may opt to buy your Pilates mat before going to your Pilates class. Pilates mats are generally thicker than yoga mats. These Pilates mats are available in a lot of fitness stores and online shops. However, the studio or center typically provides all the necessary Pilates equipment, including mats.

You may want to bring your water bottle to keep yourself hydrated during the session. Pilates workouts, although low-stress, can still be quite tiring. You may also want to bring your face towel to wipe off your sweat during the exercise.

What to Wear

Pilates involves various movements that you usually have to hold for a few seconds. Thus, you must wear something you can freely move in. Find something comfortable that won't give you a difficult time when you stretch or move.

It may also be a good idea to find clothes that fit you well enough for the instructor to appreciate your form, making sure that you are doing the correct techniques. Also, Pilates is usually performed barefoot. Thus, you don't need to wear any specific shoes or footgear when going to class. It is also best to avoid wearing any unnecessary accessories, such as bracelets or dangling earrings. You may also want to wear a headband or a clip to keep your hair away from your face.

Warming Up

Before starting Pilates or any form of exercise, it is necessary to warm up and stretch your muscles first. Doing this prevents you from acquiring any injury during class. A good idea would be to practice some simple moves, such as the pelvic curl. It is also important to psych yourself up by doing sequential breathing exercises.

Self-Evaluation

When doing Pilates exercises, it isn't enough for you to copy what you see. It is also important for you to know how to evaluate yourself. A great instructor can teach you the proper techniques when doing a Pilates workout. Another good idea would be to use mirrors so that you can see yourself while doing the exercises. Most studios have mirrors on the walls to help you out.

Now you are ready to begin Pilates! Enjoy!

Beginning Mat Pilates

Beginning Mat Pilates

Before beginning any Pilates exercise, it is a good idea to practice some basic Pilates exercises. This can also serve as a warm-up for your body before working out.

Sequential Breathing Exercises

One of the foremost principles of Pilates is proper breathing. A full breath accompanies every Pilates exercise. Breathing deeply requires you to exhale all the air out of your lungs and breathe as deeply as you possibly can. You have to allow the air to expand your lungs and open up your muscles in the back and the sides.

Sequential breathing exercises teach you the proper way of breathing for your Pilates workout. Start by sitting down on the floor with your spine straight and your shoulders relaxed. You may feel heavy like your weight is falling. Breathe in deeply and slowly, letting the air fill your chest and feeling your diaphragm, back muscles and sides expand. Keep your shoulders relaxed and don't let them rise. Hold your breath for a few seconds, and then exhale slowly, pulling in your muscles and releasing the air.

Pull in the abdominals

Another important exercise before starting your Pilates workout is pulling in your abdominal muscles. This can help improve your core strength, which is necessary for Pilates exercises. Improving your abdominal muscles provides better support to the spine and stability to the rest of the body.

Pulling in your abdominal exercises requires you to utilize your pelvic muscles, abdominals, and your back. Using your pelvic muscles is similar to Kegel exercises for women. Pull up your pelvic muscles to the center of your body. Next, pull in your lower abdominal muscles, gradually working your way up to the center, and eventually pulling in your upper abdominal muscles, too. While doing these, the back must remain straight, providing strength to the spine.

Starting the Workout Proper

A Pilates mat workout typically begins with the individual lying supine on the mat, keeping her knees bent and her feet flat on the mat. From there, several exercises can be accomplished. Some basic exercises include the pelvic curl, the spine stretch, swimming, and the hundred.

The Pelvic Curl

The pelvic curl can serve both as a warm-up for the spine and as part of the exercise proper. First, lie down and inhale and exhale, remembering to pull in your abdominal muscles at the same time. On your next breath, slowly lift your buttocks, followed by your hips and your spine. Rest your weight on your shoulders, keeping a straight line from your hips up. When you let out your breath, slowly lower your spine, hips, and buttocks to the floor.

The Spine Stretch

The spine stretch allows you to open up your back muscles and your hamstrings. First, sit up straight, with your legs outstretched in front of you and your feet pointing to your head. Place your arms in front of you, keeping them straight. Inhale deeply. Try reaching your toes as you slowly exhale. Once you have fully stretched, exhale some more. Finally, return to the sitting position.

Swimming

Swimming is a good way for toning the abdominal muscles, the back, and the buttocks. First, lie prone on the mat, with your arms straight over your head. Next, slowly lift your left arm and right leg. Alternate that by slowly lifting your right arm and left leg.

The Hundred

The hundred focuses on the powerhouse of the body, providing core strength and coordination. First, lie straight on your back and inhale deeply. While exhaling, simultaneously curl your chin and neck down to your chest and lift your legs, keeping them straight. You will form a sort of V shape. Hold the position for 5 short breaths. Finally, slowly release your body down.

Cool Down

Cooling down is just as important as warming up. It slows down your heart rate, preventing you from fainting. It also helps your muscles recover from the stress of the exercise you have just finished. Cooling down requires you to keep moving, but gradually slow down your movements. Again, breathing exercises are used in cooling down.

There are many other Pilates exercises that you can do, depending on your level of fitness and we cover all of them in-depth in upcoming chapters.

You can also modify your workout, especially if you have a certain disease. Remember to put in variations to your workout so that your body won't get bored with it. Have fun doing Pilates!

Props and Equipment for Pilates

Most Pilates exercises can be accomplished on the floor, with only a Pilates mat. However, some exercises require certain Pilates equipment and devices to produce a more effective Pilates workout.

Pilates Equipment

There are numerous items of Pilates equipment available on the market today. Some of the more common Pilates equipment include the Pilates Reformer, the Pilates Chair, the Pilates Cadillac, the Pilates Spine Supporter, and the Pilates Barrel.

Let's take a look at some of them:

Pilates Reformer

The Pilates Reformer is a special piece of Pilates equipment composed of smaller components, allowing an individual to do over a hundred Pilates exercises on it. It is made up of a gliding platform, where a person can stand, sit, kneel, or lie down; and a foot bar, where a person can push off using the upper or lower extremities. The springs may be adjusted, depending on your progress. The Reformer provides postural alignment while allowing you to work and lengthen your upper and lower extremities. The Reformer is available in various colors and finishes, with a price range of $2000-$4000.

Pilates Chair

The Pilates Chair is composed of a seat and a foot pedal. Different models contain either four or five springs, supporting the lower back while working out various muscle groups. Additional features have been added to the Pilates Chair, such as handles and rotational discs. Pilates chairs cost approximately $700-$1200.

Pilates Cadillac

The Pilates Cadillac, also known as The Rack, is composed of an elevated piece of board and a metal frame, where different bars, springs, and straps are positioned. It was previously used in the rehabilitation of bedridden patients but is currently being used for a range of workouts, from simple exercises to advanced acrobatics. Over 80 exercises can be done on the Pilates Cadillac.

Pilates Spine Supporter

The Pilates Spine Supporter is a piece of equipment shaped like a half-moon used to stabilize the spinal column during Pilates exercises. This is especially useful for people with bad backs, and can also help in establishing the proper form for back and abdominal exercises. Pregnant patients are also advised to use this device. The Pilates Spine Supporter typically costs around $150.

Pilates Barrel

The Pilates Barrel is a piece of semi-circular equipment used to support the back, neck, or hips. The equipment allows an individual to accomplish deep stretching exercises. The size of the barrel varies, depending on your body type. The Pilates Barrel costs approximately $130-$230.

Pilates Props

Smaller equipment or props may also accompany a Pilates workout. The small sizes of these accessories make them portable, especially for travelers. By combining various Pilates props, one can perform a complete workout. Pilates props include the Pilates Ball, the Pilates Resistance Band, and the Pilates Circle.

Pilates Balls

One of the most popular Pilates accessories, the Pilates Ball requires an individual to continuously balance himself while sitting or lying down on it. This also helps improve a person's stability and motor control. Pilates balls may be circular or oblong and come in various diameters, usually ranging from 55-75 cm. They are usually bought at around $25-$40, including the air pump.

Pilates Resistance Bands

Pilates Resistance Bands are composed of a piece of stretchable latex material hooked to two handles. The components may be separated, making the resistance bands quite portable. The bands provide varying resistance while working out, and allow an individual to work most of the muscle groups in the body. The latex strips cost approximately $5-$10.

Pilates Circle

The Pilates Circle is made up of flexible plastic forming a circular shape. The Pilates Circle can be used for abduction-adduction exercises to help tone the arms and legs. Pilates Circles have different diameters and a varied range of resistance. They also come in various colors. The Pilates Circle cost about $30-$60.

When looking for Pilates equipment, look for materials that are durable and made by one of the established Pilates equipment suppliers. This ensures that your Pilates equipment will last a long time and can be repaired if necessary.

This equipment provides a variety to your Pilates sessions, and can effectively accompany your mat exercises. Most of this equipment, however, requires adequate guidance before use. A wide assortment of books and videos can be utilized to provide guidance when using any of these devices. A qualified trainer can likewise help you establish the proper form while learning more exercises.

What is Contrology

Contrology: Strength, Flexibility, and Endurance from the Core

Contrology was the term used by Joseph Pilates, the German boxer cum circus performer who developed this form of exercise in the early 1900s.

If you recall from our earlier discussion in chapter one Pilates developed Contrology after being captured in England during the onset of World War II. He developed a method of exercise to help rehabilitate the patients from injuries and diseases while he was detained as a suspected foreign enemy. Pilates used crude instruments that were available at that time to help facilitate the effectiveness of his exercise method.

The basic principle of Contrology is to maximize even the slightest movement of the body to build strength, endurance, and flexibility. Joseph Pilates integrated the use of proper breathing in Contrology to build stamina and strength from the inside as well.

To this day, Contrology is being practiced and was appropriately renamed Pilates, after the name of the man who developed the exercise regimen. The popularity of Pilates is widespread in the United States as well as in Asia and Europe because of the positive effects it has brought to many of its practitioners.

The main foundation of Pilates is centered on the six main principles that integrate body movement and mental control. These are:

BREATHING

When Joseph Pilates developed Contrology, one important aspect of the exercise was breathing. He always taught his students to use deep breathing while doing the exercise to improve the lungs and chest muscles.

Breathing is also important in contrology because it guides every movement. The inhaling and exhaling of air work in conjunction with every physical movement.

CENTERING

Centering is where contrology involves focus and the control of movement from the body's core. The main source of energy while doing Contrology or Pilates is situated in the area between the pubic bone and the lower ribs.

CONCENTRATION

This principle integrates the use of mind and body while doing the exercise. Concentration helps in achieving the maximum advantage of contrology without maximizing movement.

Joseph Pilates uses concentration as an important principle of Contrology to put forth the necessary focus on the exercise to achieve the desired result.

CONTROL

Muscular control is referred to in this section. In contrology, it is essential to control the muscles even in the slightest movement. Controlling the muscles helps build strength and resistance as you advance.

FLOW

Flow pertains to the execution or how the exercises are done. Joseph Pilates wanted to minimize movement while maximizing its efficiency and full-body effects; hence he incorporated the use of flowing movements instead of the common strenuous exercises known to man. Flow also pertains to the energy that passes from one point of the body to the other as you exercise.

PRECISION

In contrology, it is vital to be attentive when carrying out the movements. Contrology aims to have the proper placement and alignment of one body part to another as you course through with every movement.

During Joseph Pilates' time, Contrology was considered a necessity to help heal the injured. But as the years passed, fitness-conscious folks have embraced this form of exercise.

80 PLUS YEARS OF CONTROLOGY/PILATES

When Joseph Pilates taught contrology in New York, from 1926 to 1966, many of his students became contrology teachers; thus, passing the knowledge and experience on to the next generations.

The classic style of Contrology was used by the first wave of Contrology teachers, those who were directly taught by Joseph Pilates himself. Some of the later waves of Contrology students have integrated their style of Contrology exercises based on their research and experience, making it uniquely their own.

Nowadays, the latest version of Contrology, as we all well know as Pilates, has improved. It is also referred to as contemporary contrology.

CONTROLOGY/PILATES FOR THE YOUNG AND OLD

Since Contrology was developed as a rehabilitation exercise for the injured, the need for slow and non-impact movements were used. The exercise was developed to strengthen the muscles during healing and to allow flexibility.

The beauty of the nature of Contrology is that it is suitable for all ages. It is good for the active and the sedentary person. Incorporating Contrology with other sports and fitness activities also enhances the body's condition and inner strength.

BENEFITS OF CONTROLOGY (PILATES)

Long-time Contrology practitioners would have many different answers when asked about the benefits they get from this form of exercise. Below are just some of the most common benefits that you can get from Contrology:

1. Improves posture and mobility
2. Helps prevent injuries
3. Enhances inner strength
4. Improves body's flexibility
5. Improves alertness
6. Enhances mind and body coordination
7. Improves the abdominal muscles
8. Improves the circulation
9. Helps develop sleeker and firmer muscles
10. Improves body alignment
11. Increases energy levels
12. Helps reduce stress and fatigue
13. Helps improve sleeping habits

Pilates for Rebuilding Strength and Flexibility

Rebuilding Strength and Flexibility through Post-Surgery Rehabilitation and Pilates

Remember that the development of Pilates was solely aimed at the recovery of the injured and sick during World War II. When Joseph Pilates developed this form of exercise it was to rehabilitate patients with injuries. The slow movements and coordinated breathing were integrated to achieve healing, flexibility, and strength.

When Joseph Pilates introduced the exercise in America, his then-classical method became more conventional over the years as more students became interested and involved. And for more than 80 years, the Pilates method of exercise has helped many students achieve the flexibility and inner strength that it promises.

With the popularity of Pilates as a low-impact and slow-natured exercise, patients who have undergone both major and minor surgeries have opted to incorporate Pilates in their rehabilitation. It sounds too good to be true, doesn't it?

You see, our body can regenerate cells, recover from illnesses, and become tolerant to diseases given the right conditions. Pilates utilizes the natural capabilities of our body to develop strength and endurance, hence recovery.

Patients recovering from different types of surgery can opt to undergo Pilates sessions when their wounds have completely healed and with the guidance of their attending physicians. The medical world has opened its doors to alternative ways of rehabilitating recovering patients, which makes it easier for Pilates teachers and professionals to help patients.

Patients recovering from heart surgery, knee surgery, lumbar fusion graft [a procedure done for patients with scoliosis], joint repairs, and others can benefit from Pilates. Since the main purpose of Pilates is to rehabilitate the injured, it has now proved to be one of the best methods of rehabilitating and recovering the strength of patients.

How can patients benefit from Pilates?

- The non-impact and slow nature of this exercise helps strengthen the patient's muscles and bones while developing an increase in flexibility and endurance.

- Pilates concentrates on the repair of the injury while rehabilitating the whole body to enhance healing.

- Proper breathing is one of Pilates' basic principles and it helps oxygenate the blood and improves circulation which enhances the healing process.

- Pilates also helps promote resistance and decrease pain due to the enhanced circulation of the blood during the actual session.

- Mind and body coordination, as the basic principle of Pilates, helps promote faster healing, resistance, and a decrease in pain, and endurance.

Things to consider when opting for rehabilitation and recovery with Pilates:

If you are recovering from major surgery, it usually takes time to heal the wounds, but the benefits you will get from rehabilitation with Pilates are certainly long-term. You can opt for a private session first with a private Pilates instructor or you can go to a Pilates Center and request a convenient schedule.

Opting for a private or personal session enables you to recover at your own pace. Discuss your plan for recovery with your instructor before embarking on your course of exercise so you both have a clear picture of what you wish to accomplish.

Normally, you will start with the basic movements using the mat. And as you increase your inner strength and flexibility, you may opt to use a Pilates machine that is right for you.

Once you have restored your pre-surgery strength, it is time to decide whether to join a group or use a more advanced Pilates machine. Ask for your doctor's approval before the session, especially if you are a recovering heart surgery patient. Ask for an assessment from your attending physician and inform your Pilates instructor about it before you give it a go.

If you have been utilizing Pilates for your post-surgery recovery, you might as well consider doing it long-term. Remember that Pilates increases strength, flexibility, and endurance, so there is no turning back after a long-term period of using it for your recovery.

Long-term Pilates helps patients to continuously increase and reach a steady level of strength, thus preventing the occurrence of other injuries.

The long-term also means a routine to keep the patient's body in shape while building and maintaining flexibility and strength.

Other benefits of long-term Pilates are:
- Resistance and tolerance to pain
- Muscle repair and strength
- Relieves patients from stress and anxiety due to surgery
- Improves well-being
- Promotes calmness

Pilates - Exercises and Benefits Part One

A Brief Peek at Exercise Tasks in Pilates

Pilates is truly one of the popular physical fitness systems nowadays. Many gyms and fitness centers are rolling out or offering Pilates classes for members. Pilates aficionados assert that the system is very helpful in providing balance for the body and the mind.

We live in a rapidly changing environment. Contrary to the lifestyles of ancient people who were more inclined to physical labor, today's generation is different because most jobs are sedentary. Thus, people need other activities that incorporate exercise to keep their blood flowing smoothly, burn calories, and flex those muscles for resistance.

Pilates helps people not just achieve their physical goals, the exercise also helps them improve body balance and overall posture. Specifically, Pilates is aimed at helping people develop a balance between aligning the spine and breath inhalation and exhalation.

But, just like all other special physical exercises, Pilates has its own set of styles and mechanics. To be able to acquire and maximize the full benefits of the activity to the body, it is advisable to learn the special tasks and body positions used in the practice of Pilates. Just like in all exercises, coordination of physical stress and breathing is the key to the effectiveness of the exercise.

Footwork in Pilates

More emphasis is given to footwork in Pilates. That is because muscles in the legs and the lower part of the body are the main focus and source of strength in the exercise. You will be moving your body muscles, but the biggest muscle group, which consists of the foot and lower body muscle group, dictates control and balance.

To begin with, you must observe proper posture and procedure when doing footwork in Pilates. Be aware of the recommended first position before you proceed to start the Pilates exercise session. You could choose to try out the monkey on a branch, which is a relaxing initial footwork position.

However you choose to start your Pilates session, you must make sure your heels are in a parallel position. Your toes must also be parallel to each other. Doing so will enable you to easily do an internal rotation, which will be necessary for some parts of the exercise.

There are also lunge exercises that are incorporated in modified form in Pilates. Examples are the calf raises, where the leg muscles are exercised and flexed. You could also put your body weight on a single leg on your heel or your toe.

You could choose to do a variety of Pilates footwork tasks. You could take in a combo or single exercise. The combo exercises are naturally consisting of a set of leg exercises infused and integrated into a Pilates exercise. An example of this is the ballet combo, which is an integration of several ballet movements specially modified for Pilates. There is also the sleeper style of exercise for Pilates.

Supine positions in Pilates

Other than the footwork, you should also be aware of the different supine or lying positions when doing the exercise. Such exercises will help the body achieve total relaxation. Take note that while the body is in a relaxed state during supine positions, movements still are energy-consuming to achieve the benefits of regular exercise.

Such positions include 'Chicken Wings' (for the arm portion of the body), 'Lat Pulls' (for the lateral region of the body), 'Angels' (similar to Chicken Wings that target the chest and arm regions), 'The Hundred', 'Frog Extensions' and triceps exercises during Pilates. 'Levitation Verite' is also among them, as well as the short spine stretch.

If you want to attain the full benefits of the supine positions, you must make sure there is full coordination of the overhead portion of the body and the back. Breathing is, of course, another important factor.

Rowing movements

If you are observing Pilates exercises, you must have noticed that there are tasks that resemble movements in rowing. Such movements are recommended and required in every Pilates session because they facilitate proper coordination between breathing and different muscle groups all across the body.

Rowing movements in Pilates include 'Hug a Tree', 'Salute', 'Modified Front Rowing', 'Front Rowing', 'Round Back', and 'Flat Back Hinge'. Executing such exercises will help maximize and attain the intended overall effects on the body of Pilates.

If you take the time to get to know Pilates and its benefits better, you will understand and be able to attain the advantages of doing the exercise system regularly. This will ultimately lead to better health.

Pilates - Exercises and Benefits Part Two

Bringing Health Back through Pilates

Pilates has become so popular in the fitness industry because of the long range of benefits it offers to those who diligently incorporate it into their lives. Many people testify to the life-changing results of such a program and these aficionados often do Pilates exercises that target specific body parts that they like to work on.

A tailor-fit Pilates workout

Knowing the specific benefits associated with each set of Pilates exercises is essential in maximizing your Pilates workout. To do this, you can start with a list of general benefits that Pilates offers and then narrow it down to your specific choices.

After having chosen the specific benefit(s) you want to get out of your Pilates workout it is the time that you engage in a specific exercise that gives you the advantage. Take for example the following exercises which are known to have specific rewards for those who incorporate them into their workout.

Back strengthening Pilates

There are a good number of exercises that can remedy back problems such as the Pilates Reformer or Long Box; the Roll Down; and the Plank or Long Stretch Series. These three are all beneficial to one's back, however, each offers a slightly different but related benefit compared to the other.

If you wish to strengthen your back muscles and would like to ensure that you have good spine alignment then the Pilates Reformer or the Long Box exercise is advisable.

To do this, you must lie down on your stomach making sure that your chest is positioned off the front side of the low box. With one strap in each hand, bring the straps down to the level of your hips. As you pull down on the straps, bring your head and chest up using strength from your abdominal muscles. Release the straps while slowly exhaling. To add intensity to this workout, incorporate triceps extensions after you pull on the straps.

Another progression of this workout begins with Chest Expansion, followed by a series of exercises that includes La Croix, Rotator, The Queen, Pulling Ropes, The Tee, Backstroke, Balance Point, Dead Hang, Hamstrings, Charlie Chaplin stance, Swimming, Rocking Swan, and finished off with the Grasshopper.

Getting to the core

Another way to improve the condition of your back is by strengthening your abdominal muscles, this being the core, center, or powerhouse of your body. Pilates' core exercises refer to those that target the support structure of the body: the upper and lower abdominal muscles and the back muscles. Take note that the back is better supported by strong abdominal muscles and acts as a force that straightens the back and rewards the person doing the exercise with an improved posture.

Roll-down Pilates is a good example of a core exercise. There are two popular ways of doing a roll-down, one is done standing up and the other while lying down on your back.

For the wall roll-down, adopt a sitting stance with your back straight against the wall and your knees slightly bent and spaced a foot apart (or shoulder-width apart). Slowly let your chin drop to your chest and your back follow this direction. Make sure you do this motion one vertebrate at a time. While you are doing this, keep your hands loose and relaxed, and continue doing the roll down until your hands are touching the floor.

Repeat the roll-down a good four to six times per set. A good follow-up on this exercise would be a reverse teaser or a mermaid.

Finally, do some advanced Pilates with the Plank or the Long Stretch series which involves a "u" Pull, Around the World Up Stretch, Down Stretch, Arabesque, FTD Florist, Elephant, Forward Bend Stretch, and wrap it up with a Long Back Stretch. This set of exercises is also known to strengthen the core, more specifically to build endurance in the muscles involved.

Regardless of which type of Pilates exercise you choose to do, you must always remember to observe proper form. The above three are just some examples of Pilates exercises that greatly benefit one's back, there are lots more, and every single one can offer you something good for your body.

Pilates - Exercises, and Benefits
Part Three

Pilates as a Way of Life

More and more people are enrolling in Pilates classes, and the news that celebrities are doing Pilates to keep fit makes it much more appealing. Never mind that this isn't a cardiovascular exercise, gone are the days when only hi-impact aerobics and physically strenuous activities were believed to bring about weight loss.

This has become the day and age where body sculpting and toning are believed to be as important as cardiovascular endurance and strength. This time, muscle endurance is said to play a key role in the physical and mental well-being of people who engage in intense workouts. Not to mention, the ability of these exercises to contribute to weight loss.

The long list of benefits associated with Pilates includes flexibility, increased strength and stamina, balance, good posture, muscle toning, and improved body coordination to name a few. To some, Pilates isn't simply a way to look good and feel great. Some turn to Pilates to improve their lives by improving certain health and body conditions. Such is the case with those who have bad backs.

Saving your back

Pilates is known to develop your core muscles (abdominals and back). However, the different exercises weren't created equal and each offers a unique approach to achieving the desired results. Take for example the Stomach Massage, the Knee Stretch, the Kneeling Exercise, and the Kneeling Side Arm. These four all use your abdominal muscles, but since they are done differently the specific muscles in your core are also used in various ways.

The stomach massage isn't an ordinary massage that involves kneading of the stomach, as you would do in a body massage. The massage takes place inside when your muscles are at work while you do this exercise. You may choose to do this exercise while you are on a reformer if you are sitting on a ball, or even when on the floor.

On the mat, sit down with your back slightly rounded, and your knees bent and aligned with your shoulders while your toes are resting ever so slightly on the mat. Your body weight shouldn't be resting on your toes, instead, you must use your core muscles to balance yourself with as little weight on your toes as you can manage. Stretch your arms in front of you, and when fully balanced twist to one side while straightening your back and your hips still in the original position, with one arm stretched to the direction of the stretch and turned out as if to embrace a huge tree but keeping your arms somewhat on a 180-degree line. Hold the stretch and then twist to the other side repeating the same movement, with your lower body intact and your upper body as the main source of movement.

Additional legwork

To add a little leg movement while still working on abdominal endurance, do a Knee Stretch. This is done with your legs in a Pilates stance as you lie on your back, and balance while reaching for the ankle of one leg with the other leg outstretched. Prepare to shift legs, while stretching the spine before reaching for the other leg. Observe proper breathing while doing this exercise, inhaling as you pull a leg towards you and exhaling as you shift your legs.

Kneeling Pilates may also sometimes include several other exercises in a set, such as a chest expansion, arm circles, salute, and a kneeling backbend.

A more challenging version of this exercise is the kneeling side arm, which starts with your hands and knees on the mat as if your body were a table. Then slowly outstretch one leg behind you to your side and the arm opposite this leg is also outstretched to your side at shoulder level. Return your leg and arm to the starting position and repeat with the other leg, do this until you've completed ten repetitions on each leg.

If you intend to do one after the other, make sure you get enough rest during intervals so as not to fatigue your muscles. More importantly, observe proper form in every exercise that you do.

Pilates - Exercises, and Benefits Part Four

Hollywood Legs Made Attainable with Pilates

The Pilates exercise method is a popular non-aerobic exercise that involves stretch-like movement partnered with proper breathing techniques. A long range of benefits is associated with this highly acclaimed exercise that has been followed by both young and old alike.

Trying out for yourself what Pilates is all about is the key to understanding the buzz behind this exercise. At present, it is no longer made available exclusively to the Hollywood elite and is offered by several local gyms and certified Pilates trainers from all over the globe. It has become a globally recognized exercise that intends to stay for generations to come.

Variations in Pilates

There are three levels of Pilates exercises, and this includes programs for the beginner, the intermediate, and the advanced. The more controlled the movement in the exercise, the easier it is for a person to move from one level to another. The common practice in improving one's way of doing Pilates is by the execution of a combination and series of both easy and challenging exercises that belong to each group.

Moreover, some exercises are used by Pilates practitioners regardless of their level of expertise in this regimen.

Examples of this exercise enjoyed by beginners and more advanced Pilates followers include variations of the Leg Stretch and the Long Spine Stretch.

Doing the Leg Stretch
Although termed "Leg Stretch," this exercise uses several muscles not necessarily isolated to your leg muscles. The whole concept behind
Pilates exercises are the strengthening of the core, and this refers to the powerhouse of the body, the abdominal and back muscles. This is why most if not all of the exercises involve the use of the core muscles regardless of the body part being exercised. The core is where you are expected to get
your strength and balance, and by using those muscles in almost all exercises you are expected to have total body improvement and wellness.
To start with the Leg Stretch, you must lie on your back with both knees to your chest. Make sure that your back is in the neutral position on the mat while you balance yourself with the use of your core muscles. Next, bring your head up as you would in an abdominal crunch, and then extend your legs outward at a somewhat 45-degree angle while maintaining the position of your spine and exhaling as you lengthen your legs. Repeat as desired.
Moving on to the Long Spine Stretch
Looking long and lean can't be achieved by just one exercise, and is attainable only after several repetitions of various Pilates exercises. In addition to the Leg Stretch, the Long Spine Stretch is also known to help elongate the body. Unlike the Leg Stretch, the Long Spine Stretch starts with a sitting position and your legs spread a little

wider than your shoulders with feet flexed, and your arms outstretched to your front (as if to reach far out in front of you). In this exercise, you must be conscious of the control of your front and back and be sure to use your core muscles during the stretch at all times. Progress from the starting position to collapsing your spine even more as you reach further forward with your head and shoulders still relaxed. Remember that you are reaching forward not merely by an extension of your arms, but by lengthening your body using your core.

In no time, you will have the so-called unattainable Hollywood legs just by religiously doing your Pilates exercises. However, before you start any stretching on the mat, you should find a certified Pilates trainer who can keep a watchful eye on you while you are learning the ropes of Pilates.

There are several videos and fully illustrated Pilates exercises available on the market, but if you are unsure of your body coordination and ability to follow and adopt proper form and technique then a few sessions with a trainer or a Pilates facility near you will do the trick. Soon, you can do Pilates exercises on your own in the comfort of your own home.

Pilates - Exercises and Benefits Part Five

Keeping Pilates Affordable and Accessible
As we have repeated throughout our instructions, Pilates is all about a series of exercises that involve proper breathing techniques along with the use of key muscles to build endurance and strength. It is because of this that those who regularly do Pilates also experience a series of benefits. The benefits vary from flexibility to increased muscle tone to improved posture and spine alignment.

Ever since Pilates was founded in the 1920s, this system of exercise has evolved and proven itself as a classic exercise rather than a craze or trend. Today, the benefits of Pilates are enjoyed by several people including but not limited to housewives, athletes, businessmen, the working class, and even as elite as Hollywood celebrities and Blue-blooded Royalty.

The expenses involved
The initial impression of Pilates is that of an expensive hobby or exercise activity. Contrary to popular belief, however, the benefits of Pilates can be experienced even by those on a limited budget. The vision of its founder Joseph Pilates is that the average person could do the exercise as long as he has a mat. In some cases, you can even replace a mat with a towel if ever you need to improvise.

For those who can afford to buy special Pilates equipment, the wide range of exercises and their variations depending on the kind of equipment is easily accessible to them. Fortunately, the popularity of Pilates has enabled the market to introduce gyms or facilities with special equipment that can be used by groups or specifically their members. What this does is minimize the costs involved in experiencing the benefits of a wide range of

Pilates exercises to their fullest.

You may choose to review the chapter on Pilates equipment to refresh yourself on the different types of tools available. In Part Six we will expand on the use of this equipment.

In addition, affordable classes offered by certified Pilates trainers promote socialization and motivation for the continuity of Pilates workouts, not to mention it's widespread across the globe.

The special equipment

Through the years, manufacturers have come up with modern designs of Pilates equipment. The evolution of such tools was also a result of advancements and recent development in Pilates.

Some of this equipment includes the Long Box, Short Box, Split Pilates Chair, The Reformer, The Plank, and so much more. Each has a different use and its own set of exercises that can be done with it. Some are more versatile than others while some are simply limited in their use.

Variations in Pilates equipment are common, and such is the case with the Long Box and the Short Box. These two are used in addition to The Reformer and are placed on top of it for elevation. The boxes are more or less one foot tall and using them brings about a more advanced and isolated

Pilates workout.

The Short Box

Several exercises can be done using the Short Box and these include the Round Back Roll-down, Flat Back Hinge, Old Man at the Gym, Up and Over a Barrel, Twist Round Back, Spear a Fish or Around the World, Climb a Tree, Side Sit-Ups, Semi-Circle, Tendon Stretch, Tendon Stretch Around the World, and Prancing to name a few.

Another exercise that can be performed with the use of a Short Box is called Climbing the Tree. This exercise begins with a sitting position atop the Short Box, and one foot is on the strap of the Reformer while another is extended to the front. The stretch happens when the student leans backward while the extended leg remains at its starting position. After holding this pose,

The student slowly assumes the first position by also utilizing the straps, and this can be repeated with the opposite leg extended in front.

A beginner who experiences the Short Box Series for the first time may need a few mat exercises for warm-up. The main challenge of the stretches involved overcoming any fear of falling off the box, and this is why the core must be used at all times so that balance may be achieved.

Remember, you need not buy your own Short Box just so you can experience this new level of Pilates. There are several gyms and Pilates

facilities that have adequate equipment including the Short Box, and all you have to do is enroll in the one nearest you.

Pilates - Exercises and Benefits Part Six

The Discipline behind Pilates

Pilates is grounded in six basic principles namely Concentration, Control, Centering, Deep Breathing, Precision, and Following Movement. The combination of these six key elements makes Pilates what it is today:

a popular muscle strengthening and conditioning that borders on discipline and hard work.

There may be other similar exercises on the market today, but it is these six principles that make it unique from the rest. In some cases, other exercises may also practice these six principles, but the interplay of these six in the execution of Pilates gives this much sought-after exercise a category of its own.

The big six concentration refers to the focus needed to carry out the exercise and is used to achieve control of body movement in each Pilates exercise. Meanwhile, Centering refers to using one's center or core muscles for each exercise while observing Deep Breathing. Proper breathing in Pilates is essential for muscle endurance, and a good flow of oxygen is needed to carry out the exercises properly.

This is also essential in achieving the next factor which is precision, or the mastering of the exercise movements by proper form. Quantity rather than quality is the concept behind Precision. Lastly, the following movement refers to the flow of the exercises as one fluid and continuous motion.

While you are on the mat or the reformer, practicing these six key concepts isn't something that you can do individually. More often than not, each movement requires the combination of most if not all of the six key principles. This can be mastered through practice, and the art of furthering your Pilates workout is based on the successful enforcement of all six in every Pilates set that you do.

The core principles

Mastering these six factors is the reason why Pilates keeps it challenging and interesting for both novice and professional practitioners alike. Moreover, the practice of one principle leads to the achievement of another.

To further illustrate the execution of these six elements, take for example the Pilates Split Series. This is an effective exercise for toning the lower

body, including the inner and outer thighs. The upper back also benefits from this exercise through an improved posture and for some, a way to minimize pain in the lower back. This can be done by any Pilates practitioner regardless of his/her level and can be recommended for pregnant women as well.

The Split Series involves several exercises that include side splits, speed skating, back splits, front splits, and jumping prep. A more advanced version of this series includes exercises such as Thread the Needle or Star Prep, Snake

Twist, and Corkscrew.

Special Pilates equipment is usually needed for this exercise, and that is the Split Pilates Chair or the Pilates Split-Pedal Stability Chair. Some of the above-mentioned exercises may be done using this equipment, but the use of the chair isn't limited to the said exercises.

The payoff

Like most Pilates exercises, the Split Series can greatly benefit those who do the sets properly and repeatedly. Among the benefits include an improved posture, a well-toned body, and increased flexibility and muscle endurance.

Apart from this, just like any other Pilates exercise, the Split Series involves mind-and-body coordination and this sharpens the mind and ability to focus. Moreover, this set of exercises is also said to relieve physical pain in some areas of the body as well as contribute greatly to stress management and relaxation.

Pilates is popular with a varied group of people, and even those with higher needs for physical conditioning have turned to Pilates. Several athletes incorporate Pilates exercises in their training to give them an added edge. The exercises however can be adjusted to any expertise level whether you are a beginner or not. Furthermore, the use of special Pilates equipment brings your training to the next level.

Your progress in Pilates will entirely depend on how persistently you perform the exercise while observing proper form and breathing of course. You can transform your life with Pilates, and unlocking its secrets is as accessible to you as night and day.

Who Should Not Do Pilates

Is Pilates for You? Reasons Why You Should Do Pilates and Why You Should Not

Despite its recent emergence as a favorite form of exercise especially among celebrities, Pilates is not new. As we have learned, Joseph Pilates, who was a gymnast, boxer, skier, and diver, developed it in the early 1900s. Joseph Pilates had been an asthmatic child and was considered unhealthy when he

began to experiment with various physical exercises along with other disciplines involving both the body and the mind to build his strength and promote his health.

Pilates was the result of Joseph's experimentation with different exercise disciplines and meditative practices, including physical regimens practiced in early Greece and ancient Rome and yoga. He also integrated principles associated with Zen philosophy. Joseph developed and refined his techniques over 20 years.

What makes Pilates different?

Pilates is distinct from other forms of similar exercises in that it emphasizes a body conditioning method that uses muscles to perform a specific set of controlled movements that improve strength and flexibility but without the added muscle bulk. People who practice Pilates develop toned, lean, and long muscles, reduce stress, and improve their postures.

These and other physical and mental benefits made Pilates popular, especially among dancers.

The late great George Balanchine (who choreographed 'The West Side Story) and modern dance diva Martha Graham were two of the first celebrities to use the method. When an exercise program is this good and popular, how can anybody not benefit from it?

Actually, like every form of exercise, Pilates isn't for everyone. Some people shouldn't do Pilates or at least perform only certain movements but not

all. If you've been wondering whether Pilates is for you, here are reasons why you shouldn't use Pilates as part of your exercise program:

You have a back injury or your spine is misaligned.

If you're recovering from a severe injury involving your back, you shouldn't do Pilates. The movements involved in these exercises are designed to promote flexibility, something you might not be capable of doing as of yet. Many Pilates movements also require you to stretch the length of your spine, which may put unnecessary (and even risky) stress on your back.

If you must perform Pilates with the abovementioned conditions, make sure that you speak to your doctor or therapist first to eliminate any problems your exercise program may cause later. You might try to avoid performing Pilates on your own and work with a professional Pilates instructor instead to ensure that you perform the required movements correctly.

You're trying to lose a lot of weight.

As a form of exercise, Pilates is an excellent way of keeping the muscles toned and trimming off excess fat. It is highly recommended for pregnant women who find that Pilates helps them increase muscle strength and lose the baby weight after pregnancy.

However, if you are a little heavier, Pilates alone will not do the trick. You can't rely on smooth and gentle movements (even with a special Pilates apparatus) to get rid of the excess pounds. You'll need to find an effective cardio exercise program and pair it with Pilates and a healthy diet.

That way, you get to burn the fats and still don't lose your muscle tone.

You're pregnant and you've never tried Pilates before.

Most obstetricians/gynecologists will tell you that it is a bit risky to try a new exercise program during your first trimester. If you've never tried Pilates before your pregnancy, you might want to consult with your doctor first. Some of the movements may be difficult for you to execute initially. If you have your doctor's go signal, go to a special beginner's prenatal Pilates

class or have a session with a certified Pilates trainer qualified to instruct a pregnant woman.

Certain movements in Pilates require you to perform while lying on your back. Doctors discourage this especially during your second and third trimesters because this position tends to affect both you and your fetus' vascular system. This position impedes proper oxygen flow to the fetus.

You experience discomfort during Pilates class.
If you experience pain, shortness of breath, sudden and continuous increase in heart rate, back pain, dizziness, or chest pain, you shouldn't do Pilates. If you experience any of these, immediately stop, inform your instructor, and see your doctor.

Pilates for Pregnant Women

How Pilates Can Benefit Pregnant Women
Becoming pregnant means experiencing multiple changes in your body, sometimes all at the same time. That is why women need to maintain a healthy diet and exercise program to ensure that their bodies are at their optimum.

Pilates is one of the most popular exercise programs pregnant women use because it is a method of exercise that emphasizes smooth, fluid movements. It is quite popular among pregnant women because it is relaxing and works out many of the muscles in the back, abdomen, an
d pelvic area.
What makes Pilates special?
As a form of exercise, Pilates uses strength and flexibility training to encourage awareness of the body. This is combined with relaxation and breathing techniques in a specific pattern of movement that uses the muscles of the pelvic area and the abdomen. It is a gentle exercise that lengthens the muscles and calms the mind.

How does it benefit pregnant women?
Pilates, like yoga, doesn't require the fast, jarring movements often associated with other forms of exercise such as those found in an aerobics class. Unlike yoga, however, pregnant women appreciate Pilates because it

involves a dynamic combination of movements instead of simply maintaining static poses. Pilates also requires movements to be executed with few repetitions, making them easy to perform and the moves are controlled and precise.

Pilates emphasizes building strength in the areas of the abdomen and the back, areas that are essential for ensuring that the muscles that usually weaken during pregnancy are targeted.

Pilates exercises are often performed in a bent-over position, which is helpful for pregnant women by minimizing the pressure on the pelvic region and the lower back.

Pilates also encourages deep breathing, which not only promotes a feeling of relaxation but also sets the abdominal muscles in motion, particularly the transverses abdominous. This group of muscles supports the pelvic area and the lumbar spine and is particularly helpful during and after pregnancy. The breathing exercises also improve the mobility of the diaphragm, especially when its movements are limited because of the presence of the baby.

Another common problem during pregnancy that Pilates solves is back pain, often the result of a weak spine, pelvis, and abdominal muscles. By strengthening the abs, the spine becomes aligned, which will prove beneficial, especially during labor. An aligned posture helps promote safer and quicker childbirth. A strong abdomen also strengthens the pelvic floor, ensuring that the muscles are strong. Post-pregnancy helps minimize problems with incontinence.

Low impact exercise

Pilates movements are naturally gentle and low impact, so pregnant women can exercise without stressing their bodies, particularly their joints. The smooth movements also don't encourage a sudden increase in heart rate. A gentle exercise like Pilates also relieves stress, promotes hormonal balance, and lessens pregnancy symptoms like morning sickness.

Pilates stretches and tones the muscles, encouraging hip flexibility and developing stamina, an excellent way to prepare for childbirth and the conditions prevalent after childbirth. Used with accompanying apparatuses or without, Pilates exercises are effective and relatively safe for use by pregnant women.

Are there any considerations pregnant women should have when using Pilates?

Before starting a pregnancy exercise, always consult your doctor. Start with beginner levels and inform your instructor about your new condition. Not all

Pilates exercises are considered safe for pregnant women to perform and many of the movements you might be familiar with may not be suitable for you.

Also, it is important not to begin any new exercises during your first trimester or if you experience an abdominal separation during your pregnancy. You might also want to avoid Pilates if the exercises require you to maintain the positions on your back, especially during the second trimester. According to the American Council of Obstetrics and Gynecology, lying on your back might affect your vascular system.

Choose Pilates exercises that are specially developed for pregnant women and choose only the classes that are taught by certified Pilates instructors trained in teaching pregnant women.

Pilates Resources

Pilates Here, There, and Everywhere

As much as there are several Pilates exercises to choose from, the ways and means to engage in such activity are also as varied. Several factors must be considered even before you start researching and these are mainly your personal preferences and limitations.

Knowing what to look for

If you are uncertain about your preferences then it would be a good idea to ask yourself several questions. This way, you will be guided in your search, and chances are you won't be too overwhelmed if you find a lot of options to choose from. Some of the questions you should ask yourself include the following:

Narrowing down your search by answering the above-mentioned questions can save you a lot of time because you have an idea of what you are looking for, and this is far better than searching without any clue of what to look for.

Knowing where to look

Finding a Pilates training facility or trainer may be easier than you think. However, finding the best option based on your needs and preferences makes the search more challenging. You don't have to worry about it though because the popularity of Pilates has made it sufficiently

advertised and promoted, making it accessible to everyone. The Internet alone has an endless number of service providers advertising their Pilates training facilities. All you have to do is type in the keywords to start your online search. This is why you need to have a somewhat clear idea of what you are looking for. A general online search for example would simply include the keywords
"Pilates Training." Meanwhile,
A more detailed search may incl
ude an actual location where you intend to take Pilates, and keywords may include "Pilates Training" plus an actual location like New York, Paris, or wherever you intend to do Pilates.
On the other hand, several Pilates training facilities advertise in your local newspaper or magazine. If you prefer this over an online search then grabbing a copy of a recent publication is all you need. Take note of all the ads that have caught your eye and start inquiring through the phone.

If you are convinced that the place is worth checking out, then schedule a guided tour or consultation with them. Some of these facilities even offer free trial classes, so take advantage of these to be sure that you like how
They render the said Pilates classes.

Knowing whom to believe
Remember, some people will do anything to sell a product or service and most of these people don't walk the talk. Be certain that the promises these service providers include in the marketing of their Pilates training won't vanish into thin air once you've paid them. To prevent being misled

by faulty marketing do a little investigating of your own. Ask around and try to talk to people who go and train in these facilities.

In line with this, also ask people you know for referrals. They may know professional Pilates trainers who can offer competitive rates and a more personal approach to Pilates training. So don't overrule personal training of Pilates just yet. Thoroughly research first before you conclude anything; you can probably get the kind of training that you want at the price you are willing to pay—even a one-on-one!

Finally, check the credentials and professional training acquired by the trainers you wish to train under. Ask for references and lo

ok up their names in fitness organizations that oversee the certification of these trainers. It is always a good idea to double-check and to think things through. After all, Pilates is a discipline that requires hard work and perseverance, so why not start it by taking the necessary steps to ensure that you find the Pilates training best suited for you?

Appendix

What Is Pilates?
Beginning Pilates
Beginning Mat Pilates
Props and Equipment for Pilates
What is Contrology?
Pilates for Rebuilding Strength and Flexibility
Pilates - Exercises and Benefits Part One
Footwork
Supine
Rowing
Pilates - Exercises and Benefits Part Two
Long Box
Roll Down
Plank/Long Stretch Series
Pilates - Exercises, and Benefits Part Three
Stomach Massage
 Knee Stretch
Kneeling
Pilates - Exercises, and Benefits Part Four
Leg and Long Spine
Open and Close
Hollywood Legs
3-Way Hip Stretch
Pilates - Exercises and Benefits Part Five
Short Box Series

Around the World
Pilates - Exercises and Benefits Part Six
Split Series
Advanced
Who Should Not Do Pilates
Pilates for Pregnant Women
Pilates Resources